ATTITUDE OF STUDENTS TOWARDS USE OF E-RESOURCES

Ms. Qurat- Ul- Ain

Dr. Ismail Thamarasseri

About the Book

E-Resources are materials in digital format accessible electronically. This book is a outcome of a Master Level research conducted by Ms. Qurat- Ul- Ain and Dr. Ismail Thamarasseri at the Central University of Kashmir, India. This objectives of the study are: (1) To study the attitude of male and female students towards use of E-Resources in Central University of Kashmir. (2) To study the attitude of rural and urban students towards use of E-Resources in Central University of Kashmir. This research found that there is no significant difference between male and female students on attitude towards e-resources. This research found that there is a significant variation among rural and urban students of Central University of Kashmir on their attitude towards e-resources.

About the Authors

- **Ms. Qurat- Ul- Ain** holds B.Ed. and M.A. Education degrees. She is currently pursuing her Masters in English from IGNOU.

- **Dr. Ismail Thamarasseri** holds B.A., B.Ed., M.A. Sociology, M.A. English, M.Ed., Ph.D., UGC-NET and CBSE-CTET qualifications. He started his teaching career at Govt. Higher Secondary School, Cheriyamundam, Tirur, Kerala, India and later worked in Farook Group of

Educational Institutions Kottakkal, Kerala, India. Presently he is working as an Assistant Professor at Department of Education in Central University of Kashmir, India. The author can be mailed at ismailktkl@gmail.com

INTRODUCTION

We are living in an age of information explosion. Computer and other electronic resources have become indispensable tools in our society. The main function of a library is to provide information to the users. With the help of electronic resources the staff, students and the researchers can have access to the huge volume of information with speed and accuracy.

Information and Communication Technology (ICT) has been proven one of the greatest innovations in teaching and learning. ICT has received momentum due to growing explosion of the Internet. The Internet creates a medium for the millions of the people to come together and engage, thereby, to help in the creation and exchange of knowledge (Rose & Fernlund, 1997). Internet has shrinked the world into a global village. By searching a word on internet one can access to the information from around fifty million different websites (Tella, 2007). The Internet provides huge information on real time basis. It is the easiest and the chief source of information among students. The use of the internet saves time and enhances the academic performance of students (Judd & Kennedy, 2010).

The number of internet users is continuously on the rise and it touched 3.8 billion in March 2017 as per the report of World Internet Users and Population Stats, 2017. Students show high percentage of internet users as compared to general public. According to Jones (2011) there are

86% of the internet users among students as compared to 56% among general population in USA. Internet users in India were about 10% in 2011 which raised to 26 % in 2015. The percentage is expected to increase due to the *Digital India* Campaign launched by the Government of India in 2015 with the initiative to increase the internet connectivity throughout India.

There are a number of studies on the Internet usage among male and female students. Park & Choi, (2007) found that male students use more internet than female students. Despite the gender equality and constitutional safe guards of the females, the males dominated the internet usage in India. In India 71% of the internet users are males and only 29% are females which is also a cause of concern and needs to be researched on the priority basis. In the present age of information and technology, most of the university students are bent towards e-learning so it becomes inevitable to conduct a research aimed at studying the attitude of e-resource use among university students.

Information is the vital element for human beings in today's world. It has become the basic need of man unlike food, drink, dress and shelter. Since beginning the libraries have been trying to manage the available literatures. Even memories of kings, various countries and individual persons which are engraved on the clay tablets, coins and on leaves, etc. is still being managed by libraries. These rare documents are the only sources to reveal most of the hidden past of our ancient and medieval history. Invention of type writer or printing press had given momentum to keep records of day to day activities. The emergence of electronic resources has drastically revamped the status of all the libraries and information centres across the world. There has been a rapid urge of the user community to get more and more information online. The development of the ICT devices, the rapid rise of electronic databases and modern e-book technologies have altogether changed the entire scenario of informatics. The users' attitude to information is gradually shifting from the printed documents to electronic resources and thus, it has been their prerogative to know the details of the availability and organization of e-resources. Electronic information resources, in reality have become the backbone of many academic organizations. The awareness and use of electronic resources by various persons depends mainly on skills of each individual to locate discrete knowledge elements. Information explosion have increased the amount of electronic information sources available on the web. Electronic resources help to expand access, increase usability and effectiveness and establish new ways for individuals to use information to be more productive in their endeavours. Awareness of electronic resources may aid the users in keeping abreast with current developments in their respective subject fields, in contrast with print media. The use of electronic resources is necessary for users mainly because the electronic resources provide better, faster and easy access to information than information accessed through print media. Electronic resources can be relied upon for timely information which upholds the quote: right information to right user at right time.

Electronic Information Resources (EIR) has their origin in experimental computer Systems developed for the storage and retrieval of bibliographic data during the 1969. By the end of that decade some of the major bibliographic databases such as Chemical Abstracts and Index Medicus were available in magnetic tape versions that were searchable in offline batch mode. During the 1970s and 1980s, the increasing availability of this machine-readable data together with the emergence of both real-time interactive computing and computer networks enabled the online information industry to emerge. Initially the major scientific bibliography databases became available in machine-readable form. During the 1980s, Academic libraries began to transfer from card catalogues to Online Public-Access Catalogues (OPAC). OPACs became widely available; the CD-ROM emerged as an information delivery vehicle. The emergence of the World Wide Web has enabled a revolution in electronic information resources. This environment differs from the earlier situation in the following ways:

- The available information is not restricted to text but includes collection of images, audio and multimedia items so that it is more appropriate to think them as information objects rather than as documents.

- The information available is an amorphous mass to which anyone can add if they have even a limited knowledge of Hyper Text Markup Language (HTML) and thus the available information is no longer subject to quality-control mechanisms prior to publication.

- The information is not structured to facilitate retrieval, but through the hypertext links it is structured to facilitate browsing and easy moving between information objects.

- The web browser environment has continued the trend towards user friendly interfaces that was initiated by the development of CD-ROM and windows. Alongside considerable change in the type and scale of available EIR, there has been an even more remarkable change in the users of these resources. Use of EIR has moved from being an esoteric activity undertaken by information professionals, and a slowly increasing band of other professional people, to an action-undertaken everyday by countless millions around the world.

The internet sense simply as an access mechanism to the quality controlled information products made available by information aggregations such as Dialog, or publishers such as ISI and the major academic publishing such as Elsevier. A range of tools has been developed to enable retrieval of material from the web. These include a large number of search Engines, directories, gateways and portals. The search engines automatically create huge databases of items on the web. The indexing and updating of these databases is done automatically by software. It is often forgotten that even the largest of these search engines, such as Google and Alta Vista, provide access to but a small proportion of the resources available on the web. The electronic surveillance and digitization of information and its flow on broad band electronic highways facilitate the connection of home, offices, including libraries and information centres to the National Information Infrastructure (NII) for transaction of information. The need for speedy processing and retrieval of information resulted in a variety of storage media such as microfiche, floppy diskette, compact disc etc.

In the words of Says (2001), "Electronic resources are the resources that are generated through some electronic medium and made available to a wide range of viewers both on-site and off-site via some electronic transferring machine or internet. "Therefore, electronic resources in its ambit include all kinds of digital collections in the form of e-books, databases, e-journals, electronic thesis and dissertations (ETDs), e-standards and patents, e-reports, etc. Moreover, ICT has enabled the transformation of electronic information services in the forms of e-assignments, e-term papers, e-project reports in many educational institutions and Universities all across the world which impels the users' community to use electronic resources for the betterment of their academic needs. Electronic resources are regarded as the mines of information that are explored through modern ICT devices, refined and redesigned and more often stored in the cyber space in the most concrete and compact form and can be accessed simultaneously from infinite points by a great number of audience. The phrase 'electronic resources,' has broadly been defined as, "information accessed by a computer, may be useful as bibliographic guides to potential sources but, as of yet, they infrequently appear as cited reference in their own right." Electronic resources and services refer to the variety of electronic and digital sources of information available to teachers and learners within an academic context. The change in traditional document delivery services, from print to electronic, has come about very quickly and libraries and information services have undergone significant transformation in order to effectively deliver electronic resources to the academic community-resources in collaboration with Internet have become a sign of modern age being an invaluable tool for teaching, learning and research. The library and information landscape has transformed with the onset of the digital era and today traditional libraries have changed their roles to serve as 'Knowledge Centre's with priority on value added electronic information services. Academic and research institutions are focusing on how best they can facilitate research by canalizing specific information services which compliment as cutting edge technology. With the advent of globalization in the realm of education, there has been an information explosion. Most of the science and technology, academic institutions as well as R&D organizations have changed their contemporary outlooks towards the functions, operations and services. The traditional environment has been rapidly changing to an electronic one and the demand for Internet and e- resources among the academic and research community has increased manifold over the years being the most popular source of undertaking research. In the present age of information, which the world is witnessing information is held as a key resource for the economic, socio-cultural and political development of a nation. Organizations, especially academic libraries make greater use and to increase their effectiveness and competitive position. People use information more intensively in their day-to-day activities. The availability of the right information for the right user at the right time and at the right cost becomes all the more vital. The scenario has posed major challenges to the information sector whose prime function is to satisfy the complex and increasing technological advancements which are putting greater pressure on librarians. First, the technology of information work is vastly extending the scope of their work. It is now possible to gain access to and process much greater quantities of information than was possible and Internet have found increasing acceptance in library and information centers. Multimedia has shown much potential for library and information centers; and information networks have broken down time and space barriers. Secondly, user expectations are rising constantly, creating a demand for ever more sophisticated, high quality information services in academic libraries.

The academic libraries spent an enormous amount of money, expertise and other valuable electronic resources to come up to a stage where they are at present in terms of service delivery. It is true that by using a variety of Information Technology (IT) tools and techniques, library and information centres are now able to generate various in addition to performing the routine tasks. The development in Information and Communication Technology (ICT) has created revolutionary changes in all fields of knowledge. Libraries being the reservoirs of knowledge are no exception to this development. People seek information for their research, education, reference and guidance from libraries. The media of communication is developing and the format of information delivery and exchange is also undergoing rapid change. People require most up-to-date information from libraries. Hence, the technological developments have to be adopted in libraries to meet the needs of user.

E-resources: Meaning

Bavakenthy et.al (2003) in discussing the concept viewed that e-resources are resources in which information is stored electrically and are accessible through electronic systems and networks. 'E-resource' is a broad term that includes a variety of publishing models, including OPAC, online databases, e-journals, e- books, internet resources, print-on-demand (POD), e-mail publishing, wireless publishing, electronic link and web publishing, etc. In this context, the term primarily denotes "any electronic product that delivers collection of data be it in text, numerical, graphical, or time based, as a commercially available resource."

In view of IFLA ISBD (ER): An electronic resource consists of materials that are computer-controlled, including materials that required the use of a peripheral (e.g. a CD-ROM player) attached to a computer; the items may or not be used in the interactive mode. There are two types of numbers, letters, graphics, images, and sound or a combination thereof) and, programs (instructions or routines for performing certain tasks including the processing of data and programme (e.g. Online services, interactive multimedia).

Graham (2003) says that, electronic resources are the means of information that are explored through modern ICT devices, refined and redesigned and more often stored in the cyber space in the most concrete and compact from and can be accessed simultaneously from infinite points by a great number of audiences. The phrase "electronic resources", has broadly been defined as information accessed by a computer, may be useful as bibliographic guides to potential sources but, as of yet, they infrequently appear as cited references in their own right. E-resources, therefore, refer to that kind of documents in digital formats which are made available to library users through a computer based information retrieval system. The Internet is said to be the right and most extensively used channel to catch hold of the majority of e-resources through different search engines and web OPAC and, of course, some off-line databases in CD/DVD formats.

However, electronic resources have become very important these days as they are up-to-date, multi-dimensional and directional in nature and also can be accessed as well as used anywhere, crossing all geographical boundaries. Such resources add value to all spheres of human activities. Information technology has revolutionized the field of library and information science. The collection of a modern library is not restricted to print media only but libraries are actively adding e-resources to their existing collections. With the increasing cost of print publications, majority of information seekers are opting for e-resources.

Shim et al. has defined e-resources as those electronic information resources and services that user access electronically via a computing network from inside the library or remote to library. The users need not come to the library to meet all informational needs. They may use online catalogue, any web-based database, e-journal etc. which are remote from library. E-resources provide access to substantial portion of world's literature expeditiously, exhaustively, efficiently, pin-pointedly, up-to-date and authentically at a simple touch of button. Related literature for past ten years consider that electronic resources like CD-ROM, databases, online databases and e-journals are important for research and allied activities. Introduction of e-resources has exposed the learners to much more resources of information and have become an invaluable resource of current information. The value and use of information resources, particularly e-resources, have increased with the time. Therefore, the use of e-resources by users, especially by the Academic staff members of Academic institutions generally depends on skills of each user to locate discrete knowledge elements. According to the

Final Report of the American Library Association Presidential Committee on Information Literacy, the information literate user skill is being able to recognize when information is needed and have the ability to locate, evaluate, and use information resources effectively (ALAPCIL, 2001). In Nigeria, the National Universities Commission (NUC) has subscribed to a number of international and local journals and made them accessible in Nigerian Universities through its URL link @www.nigerianvirtuallibrary.comon the internet. In addition, NUC (National Universities Commission), NULIB (Nigerian University Libraries Consortium) and EIFL.NET (Electronic Information for Libraries Network) are partnering to provide electronic resources on the internet towards qualitative teaching/research in Nigerian Universities. To date, almost all the Library functional areas and services have a touch of IT; however, the depth of application varies. The University of Lagos Library is 75% networked with a total of 211 nodes within the Main Library, 124nodes at the MTN Foundation Universities Connect Project and 68 nodes recently put in place at Education Library. In order to expand access to reading materials, the Library has adopted distributed access to information resources which include: Integrated Library Systems (ILS), Online Databases, Web-Based Resources, Digital Library Collections, e-Books and e-Journals.

Sanjeev Kumar and Yogi Ashen observed that, Information professionals have long sought to comprehend what factors are relevant in encouraging a person to seek out information. More recently, a particular focus of inquiry has been on those factors that play a role in deciding to use the library's electronic resources to seek information as opposed to just surfing the Internet. These inquiries assume on even greater importance in light of the fact that more people are using the Internet to find information they need, information that is unmediated by the library. Informed library users know that libraries have resources that are more comprehensive and scholarly than most websites provide. Libraries provide access to scholarly literature that as a rule is not freely available on the web. One obstacle to the use of a library's resources, and in particular its electronic resources, is that they are not seen as being straight forward in contrast to an Internet search engine, where a single keyword search will usually result in thousands of hits, no matter what the topic, in the library, students have to choose a particular database and be more selective in the search words they use. Moreover, database subjects often overlap, with differences in dates, journal and subjects covered, and whether the material is full-text or not. In addition, the library may have a print subscription to a certain title that is not full-text electronically, or the title may be accessible full- text through another database than the one originally searched..

E-resources: Categories

Internet is a hub of worldwide information. All types of documents are available through it. Publishing industry has been heavily depending on it. To keep bibliographical control over the published information, with the help of information and communication technology, various methods have been developed and adopted by the libraries from time to time. Broadly, two types of e-resources are available to cater scholarly information needs of the users. (1) **Licensed E-Resources:** Publisher is charging some fee to access the resource, which comes under this category. Access to products from the commercial publishers is mostly available on payment. Few of the leading publishers under this category are Royal Society of Chemistry, Elsevier, Springer, Blackwell Publishing Agency, Cambridge University Press, etc. (2) **Open Source:** The list of this type of resources is quite long and it can be divided in few sub-categories like:

- **Open Access Journals:** Many of the publishers are providing free access to few of their journals and many organizations are making open access for their products.

- **Information available at Institutional Repositories:** Various Institutional Repositories are accessible to the world without any cost. For example: Institutional Repository of D-Space at the INFLIBNET (http://dspace.inflibnet.ac.in) and

Institutional Repository of Indian Institute of Science, Bangalore can be accessed freely.

- **Organizational/ Individual websites:** Organizational and Individual websites are also a source of accurate information. For example: Union Databases (books, serials and those available with Indian Universities) and other specialized databases which are being maintained and hosted by the Information and Library Network Centre (INFLIBNET) at its official website are good source of information.

- **Individual Blogs/ Professional Discussion Forums:** These are the latest and new web options on the Internet to share one's views or opinions with other fellow professionals around the world. Day by day various forums, discussion groups and blogs are flourishing with explosive speed.

- **Universal Access to e-resources:** Libraries have always served as access points for information service have evolved from the days so closed stacks, through shelf browsing and card catalogues, punch cards and OPACs to the concept of open access and institutional repositories. This historic migration has tried to satisfy the changing needs of library users, including ease of access, interaction richness, low interaction and low cost. Eisenberg (1990) remarks that, "Access is more important than ownership. The underlying issue becomes the provision of information resources in officers, hostels, classrooms, homes, etc. regardless of where the information is found".

Attitude towards e-resources

Academic libraries new live in a superior new world. The rapid advancement of information and Communication Technology (ICT) has brought revolutionary change in the information scenario giving rise to a number of options to the users' community to handle varied information sources conveniently and effortlessly. As a result, e-resources have become the lively substance to the modern library's reserves in satisfying varied needs of students, teachers and researchers with minimum risk and time. For better planning, it is vital to have knowledge on the attitudes of users towards e-resources. The library users' attitude to information is gradually shifting from the printed documents to electronic resources and thus, it has been their prerogative to know the details of the availability and organization of e-resources like online journals and databases, electronic theses and dissertations (ETDs), government publications, online newspapers, etc. in libraries. Given technology increased use, it is important to understand how technologically rich environments are influencing faculty attitudes towards e-resources access. Many factors influence attitudes.

The introduction of open access journals and other resources for instance is creating another attitudinal tendency towards e-resources. Open access is one of the cheapest route to electronic resources have grown and provided an affordable way to provide access to some journal content. Supporters of open access argue that, when academic articles, dissertations and theses are put online and open to all, it helps in fighting duplication and plagiarism of other people's intellectual works. Although the open access movement has brought access to many valuable resources, and provided libraries with an invaluable amount of resources, many open access projects still face an uncertain future.

Attitudes towards e-resources access could be attributed to problems faced when accessing e-resources. For instance in a situation where there is inadequate computer technologies to access e-resources or poor Internet connections, positive attitudes of the users could be affected. That is why the problems that affect e-resources access are addressed in higher learning institutions libraries. E-Resources are used to access information available any time on the internet. Institutions provide e-Resource section for their students, research scholars and even for faculties so that they may use them for their study related tasks and for research work. Some factors are here from which we may know that to which extent students and faculties are provided access to e-Resources section. It is also necessary that the librarian must have the sufficient knowledge of available e-Resources so that he/she may help the students and faculties for their usage.

Students' lives today are filled with technology that gives them access to information and resources 24/7. Students are able to create multimedia content and immediately share it with the world and participate in social networks where people from all over the world share ideas, collaborate, and learn new things. Outside of the classroom, students have the freedom to pursue their passions in their own way and at their own pace. Opportunities for today's students are limitless, borderless, and instantaneous (Office of Educational Technology, U.S. Department of Education, 2010) so it only logical that their learning environment should reflect their everyday lives.

Libraries have transformed into digital and virtual libraries where books, journals and magazines have changed into e-books, e-journals, and e-magazines. This has increased the global dissemination of information (Abinew & Vuda, 2013). Electronic resources such as e journals, e-books, e-databases, web resources, e-serials amongst others are easily accessible in remote areas.

Jone (2008) opined that electronic resources solve storage problems and control the flood of information, that is, print sources is being digitized. The rapid growth of new technologies has changed the communication process and reduced the cost of communication for individuals.

Electronic information resources can be defined as the electronic representation of information which can be accessed via electronic system and computer network (Johnson, Evensen, Gelfand, Lammers, Sipe & Zilper, 2012). They further buttress that electronic information sources can be seen as the most recent development in information technology and that they are available in various forms like e-books, digital libraries, online journal magazine, e-learning tutors and online test. Because of the effective presentation with multimedia tools, these e-resources have become the source of information. Electronic resources deliver the collection of information as full text (aggregated) databases, e- journals, image collections, multimedia in the form of CD, tape, internet, web technology, etc. E-resources include e-journals, e-discussions, e-news, data archives, e-mail online chatting, just to mention but a few. Electronic information source are a wide range of products going from electronic periodicals to CD-ROMs, from mailing list to databases, all of them having a common feature of being used and sometime modified by a computer (Thanuskodi, 2012). Electronic information sources are becoming more and more important for the academic community (Egberongbe, 2011). Therefore, awareness of these information resources is of paramount importance to library development in the 21st century. Awareness is knowledge about something that exists or understanding of a situation or subject at the present time based on information or experience (Ani & Ahiauzu, 2008). It can also be seen as knowledge or perception of a situation, fact, consciousness, recognition, realization, grasp and acknowledgement concern about and well-informed interest or familiarity in a particular situation or development.

Ojo & Akande (2005) opined that students' level of access, usage and awareness of electronic information resources at the University College Hospital (UCH) Ibadan, Nigeria is not high and that the major problem however identified in their study is lack of information retrieval skills for exploiting electronic resources, thus making the level of usage of resources by medical students very low. Ajuwon (2003) study on ICTs by health science students at the University College Hospital (UCH) Ibadan, revealed that students studied could not use a computer, and that the use of the database was poor, due to lack of awareness, lack of access to computers, insufficient training and high cost of provision of electronic information resources subscription. Awareness and use of electronic information resources is very important so as to keep university students alert of the available media through which they can access needed information. It is apparent that the use of these electronic information resources require special skills in information and communication technologies (ICTs) that will help students navigate the maze of resources at their disposal via telecommunications channels (Balogun, 2008). It is also imperative to understand the purpose of using electronic information resources by postgraduate students of library and information science. Awareness of the changes in technology in recent years has dramatically altered how information is accessed, stored and disseminated (Tsakomas & Papatheodorou, 2006). Whereas information provision and usage in academic libraries was previously based upon the collection of physical library materials, it is now increasingly the case that academic libraries are moving into the virtual arena. Postgraduate students in their reaction to such stimuli ought to be aware of the availability of such resources to aid them in their academic pursuit. With advances in technology and e-publishing, online test full text databases, Emerald, Science Direct, Academic Search Premier, Ebscohost, TEEEL, Oare Sciences, Hinari, Virtual Library (NUC), Online Public Access Catalogue (OPAC), Compact Disc-Read Only Memory (CD-ROM), e-books collections, e-journals covering a variety of subjects, and major bibliographic databases like AGORA and MEDLARS etc., access to information on a local, regional, national and international basis has overcome the traditional barriers of time, easy of accessibility and space (Prangya & Rabindra, 2013; Sharma, 2009). Since electronic information resources are systems in which information is are stored electronically and made accessible through electronic systems and computer networks.

Therefore, awareness is paramount if university students' are to harness these resources. Students now tend to use only what is easily accessible. Therefore, they visit the library a lot less, and, as such, discovery through serendipity is reduced. Users often prefer increased access to databases of online-referred journals and to the Web - which provides information that is up to the minute, international in scope and sometimes not available elsewhere because they see these resources as easier to access and search. Awareness is core to usage of electronic information resources. Where materials are in closed access, users' ease of access to such e-resources is by far reduced. But where they are in open access (not subscription-based), postgraduate students' find them, and make do with them for whatever reasons they need them for. The usage of EIRs in recent years has yielded positive results in the area of teaching and research and that through the use of electronic information resources, researchers, academic and students now have access to global information resources, particularly the Internet for their scholarly intercourse. Promote e-resource usage. Although, the value and use of e-resources have increased with time since users, especially in higher institutions generally depends on skills of each user to locate discrete knowledge elements. The information literate user's skill is being able to recognize when information is needed and have the ability to locate, evaluate, and use information resources effectively. Tyagi (2011) the ability to use e-resources efficiently depends on basic computer skills, knowledge of what is available and how to use it, and ability to define a research problem. How postgraduate students attain the above skills and knowledge depends on many factors, such as their disciplines, academic status and ranks, age, access. To further buttress this, Prangya and Rabindra (2013) conclude that lack of training; poor infrastructure and high cost of accessing some e-resources are the obstacles to proper and full utilization of EIRs.

The use of electronic information resources by postgraduate students in Nigerian schools comes with a couple of challenges like the nation's poor telecommunications infrastructure which has been a subject of debate to researchers and higher institutions (Adomi, 2005). In the face of poor telecommunications infrastructure, poor user skills in navigating e-resources, high cost of Internet subscription and restricted access to e-resources are also major challenges plaguing the use of electronic information resources by postgraduate students' in Nigeria universities. Well, it's pertinent to note that when postgraduate students are aware of e-resources they make adequate use of them for academic and research purposes. It is also important that for the students to make use of the resources, they ought to be skilled in information and communication technologies (ICTs) applications in other to gain independent use of various electronic information resources around the globe. Be that as it may, it has been observed that postgraduate students in Nigerian universities are confronted with various challenges relating to inadequate telecommunications' infrastructure, high cost of subscription, poor user skills, amongst others in the use of e-resources.

Electronic information is most essentially in this modern society because everyone can access everywhere. An electronic resource you can access through the internet. You can get the information when you need it. E-resources include electronic journals, electronic books, electronic thesis and online databases etc. There are many thousands of journals and books are available and the numbers of resources are added to our collections. Electronic resources are materials in digital format accessible electronically. Examples of e-resources are electronic journals, electronic books, and online databases in varied digital formats, Adobe Acrobat documents, WebPages and more. Use of e-resources permits the library to save space of library and time of the users. Today libraries are given that electronic access to a broad diversity of resources, including indexes, full-text articles, complete journals and Internet/Web resources. The availability of a multitude of electronic information resources has made a well challenge to the libraries to improve the users (Baridi & Ahmed, 2000).

FeiXu (2010) presents library with helpful information about selection criteria for an electronic resource assessment system and useful support on how to execute powerfully such a system. The Collecting of electronic resource usage is important to a library and information centres as it useful to the librarians to create more informed and well-rounded collection results (FeiXu, 2010). The library and information services are rapidly changing in the 21st century. E-resources are helpful for libraries as well as everyone and every users of the society, who are ravenous to get a variety of information through the globe and electronic resources solve storage problems and control the flood of information.

In this electronic and Internet era, users have a number of options to fulfil their information needs. They need not come physically to the library to use print formats but can stay at home or the office and access online a variety of library resources and services via networks or authentication methods at any time. Information should be accessible, authoritative, reliable, accurate, and timely. Due to the needs of faculty for high-quality information, libraries have been early adopters of electronic resources to provide information services tailored to their needs. Electronic resources have exploded in popularity and use. They can and do enable innovation in teaching, and they increase timeliness in research as well as increase discovery and creation of new fields of inquiry (Henderson & Machewan, 1997). Other reasons for faculty to use e-resources include relating to increasingly computer-literate students and keeping up to date in their fields. Users often prefer increased access to databases of online-refereed journals and to the Web - which provides information that is up to the minute, international in scope and sometimes not available elsewhere because they see these resources as easier to access and search (Dalgleish & Hall, 2000). Availability of e-resources has changed what users actually read and use. They now tend to use only what is easily accessible. Therefore, they visit the library a lot less, and, as such, discovery through serendipity is reduced. Access to e-resources has decreased the time spent searching for information. Access is only as good as the resources that can be afforded (e.g., the number of computers and existence of network systems), the ability to work with the tools, and the network infrastructure that supports rapid and convenient connections (Forsman, 1998). The ability to use e-resources efficiently depends on basic computer skills, knowledge of what is available and how to use it, and ability to define a research problem. Faculty, due to the nature of their work - teaching, research, should have ready access to information as they need to remain themselves up-to-date before they impart teaching and guidance to their taught. By their teaching styles and course requirements, they affect the use of the library's collection and students' perception of the library. Computer-literate faculty may feel more comfortable using electronic information sources and thus gain more from using them compared to those who lack Information Communication Technology (ICT) skills (Majid & Abazova, 1998). How faculty attains the above skills and knowledge depends on several factors, such as their disciplines, academic status and ranks, age, access (hardware and location) to electronic resources, and training. Factors motivating use can be, for example, what level of importance they allocate to e-journals, how much easily assessed, the way institutes provides them, the time they need t utilize for finding relevant need etc. The library plays a leading role in faculty-library relationships and in instructional services such as orientation and training in use of library resources. If efficient and effective use is to be made of library's e-resources, then user training will have to increase both in intensity and coverage. It is important to remember that the ability of library staff to keep up to date is necessary, and, therefore, training for them is crucial as well. There is a dearth of information about e- resources in the faculty. It is hoped that this study would add to the body of the existing literature on use of e-resources by to the faculty, besides encouraging further studies of this nature covering different user groups.

Availability of e-resources has changed what users actually read and use. They now tend to use only what is easily accessible. Therefore, they visit the library a lot less, and, as such, discovery through serendipity is reduced. Access to e-resources has decreased the time spent searching for information. Access is only as good as the resources that can be afforded (e.g., the number of computers and existence of network systems, the ability to work with the tools, and the network infrastructure that supports rapid and convenient connections. The ability to use e-resources efficiently depends on basic computer skills, knowledge of what is available and how to use it, and ability to define a research problem. How scientists, researchers attain the above skills and knowledge depends on many factors, such as their disciplines, academic status and ranks, ages, access (hardware and location) to electronic resources, and training. Factors motivating use can be, for example, what level of importance they allocate to e-resources, how useful they have found them, and for which purposes they use e-resources. As users of digital information, researchers place a very high value on electronic journals, but a much lower value as yet on libraries' provision of other kinds of digital resources. Increases in the scale of research, and the growth of collaborative and inter-disciplinary research teams, present challenges to libraries in seeking to provide effective services and equitable access to the researchers. And growth in the volume and scale of research, along with the development of e-research and virtual research communities, is also leading to rapid growth in the volume of digital research outputs in many different forms; these are likely to create new challenges for librarians in data management, storage and preservation. There is an urgent need for librarians and the research community to work together to clarify the roles and responsibilities of key players – at national as well as institutional level – in managing these outputs. The rapid advancement of information and communication technology has brought a revolutionary change in the information scenario and gives rise to a number of options to handle varied information sources conveniently and effortlessly. E-resources have become the most sought after modern library's reserves in satisfying varied needs of students, teachers, and researchers with minimum risk and time. Information technology has changed the world and has become one of the important tools for retrieving information. The electronic information resources have acquired a major portion of library collections. The value and use of information resources, particularly E-resources, have increased with the time. Therefore, there is necessity to make study on the different aspects of resources and the issues relating to the use of E-resources by users, more particularly by the faculty members of academic institutions

Need and Significance of the Study

The library happens to be the nucleus of information centres which supports and facilitate learning, teaching and research needs to the user communities by providing access to scholarly literature though various e-resources. Growth and change have always been predominant characteristics of the libraries. These generate collections and services within the library system. The library needs to be adapted as it responds both to the changes of the need of the users communities and to changes within the field of information technology. Hence collection of information must remain flexible enough to support to the causes of the information requirements of the users in the Library of University in a changing technological scenario. Over and above access to electronic resources principally occupy a prevalent position and the users get benefit to a good array of literature with a cost effective and affordable price. In the present days, adoptions of information technology have compelled the library to be dependent upon digital materials which could be collected through Internet on a WWW platform. The significance of the study is that it happens to be one of the leading libraries to provide e-resources services to its clienteles. Moreover, the work aims at evaluating the flexibility of this library in this fluid environment as well as their capabilities in developing a process to integrate the changes in to a standard library practice to meet the current and update demands of the users' communities. Further, the technology has changed the expectations of faculty members, their patience and their willingness to accept services that are available on demand. Electronic resources are making a significant growth as part of library collection. But without conducting a study, there is no way of knowing whether the e-resources are reliable or useful.

Keeping these in view, the present study was taken up to ascertain the current use of e-resources by the students including male and female from rural and urban locality. To the extent of the knowledge of the investigator, no study has been undertaken so far to make an assessment of the attitude of students towards the use of electronic resources in Central University of Kashmir. The advancement in ICT, the information explosion, multiple sources of information, emergence and growth of bibliographic tools, automation of library operations and introduction of sophisticated information services necessitated information literacy programs geared to the requirements of the user groups under study for the maximum utilization of electronic resources.

Statement of the Problem

Framing of research problem is the most crucial task in any research process. It requires the researcher to identify the research issue with a narrow focus; otherwise the research pursuit may be futile. To correctly define the research problem, we need to follow certain steps, and also need to understand the process of framing hypothesis, i.e., the assumptions that we want to authenticate or otherwise through our research. On the face of it, the selection of a problem may appear to be simple but when envisages the operational difficulties of putting a design into effective research; the selection of problem is not simple task but a very complex phenomenon.

The problem under investigation reads as: "Attitude of students towards the use of E-Resources in Central University of Kashmir."

Objectives of the study

- To study the attitude of male and female students towards use of E-Resources in Central

  University of Kashmir.

- To study the attitude of rural and urban students towards use of E-Resources in Central

  University of Kashmir.

Hypothesis

Any scientific study starts with the statements of a solvable problem. When the problem has been stated, the investigator offers a tentative solution in the form of testable proposition. This testable proposition is known as hypothesis. Therefore, a hypothesis is a suggested testable answer to a problem and is a testable relationship between two or more than two variables. It means what we are looking for. The task of the researcher in the view is to express presupposed concepts and belief accurately and clearly, to ascertain which of the beliefs are true and which false and if possible to define some of the concepts in terms of situation under study. The hypotheses for the present study are as under:

- There is no significant difference in the attitude of male and female students towards the use of E-Resources in Central University of Kashmir.

- There is no significant difference in the attitude of rural and urban students towards the use of E-Resources in Central University of Kashmir.

Operational Definitions of key terms

- **E-Resources:** E-Resources are materials in digital format accessible electronically.

- **Attitude:** In the present study, attitude refers to approach of students towards digital format for academic purposes.

- **Students of Central University of Kashmir:** Students who are enrolled in Central University of Kashmir and are pursuing various programmes on regular basis.

- **Gender:** Male and Female students of Central University of Kashmir.

- **Locale:** Locality from which students belong i.e. Urban and Rural locality.

Scope and Limitations

This study helps to find out use of E-Resources for the educational purpose. Hence it was felt appropriate to take up a study on the use of electronic sources by the students of university. This study may help to take up proper guidelines to keep good acquisition policy in information. Due to the paucity of time, the investigator has limited the study only to Central University of Kashmir which constitutes of various departments spread over in four campuses.

REVIEW OF THE RELATED LITERATURE

A literature review is a summary of previous research on a topic. Literature reviews can be either a part of a larger report of a research project, a thesis or a bibliographic essay that is published separately in a scholarly journal. We do literature review to understand our research problem better. It allows us to remain up to date regarding the state of research in the field and familiarizes us with any contrasting perspectives and viewpoints on the topic.

Research takes an advantage of the knowledge which has accumulated in the past as a result of constant human endeavour. It can never be taken in the isolation of the work that has already been done on the problems which are directly or indirectly related to a study proposed by a researcher a careful review of the research journals, books, dissertations, thesis and other information on the problem to be investigated is one of the important steps in the planning of any research study.

Purpose of the Review of Related Literature

Review of the related literature; besides allowing the researcher to acquaint himself with the current knowledge in the field or area in which he is going to conduct his research, serves the following specific purposes:

- The Review of the related literature enables the researcher to define the limits of his field. It helps the researcher to delimit and define his problem. To use an analogy given by Ary et al (1972, p.56) a researcher might say: The knowledge of related literature, brings the researcher up-to-date on the work which others have done and thus to state the objectives clearly and concisely.

- By reviewing the related literature the researcher can avoid unfruitful and useless problem areas. He can select those areas in which positive findings are very likely to result and his endeavors would be likely to add to the knowledge in meaningful way.

- By the process of reviewing literature, the researcher can avoid un-intentional duplication of established findings. It is of no use to repeat a study when the facts found are valid and reliable.

- The review of the related literature gives the smooth understanding of the methodology to utilize in the process of research. It helps the researcher to choose the tools and techniques to be used which have proven purposeful in the previous studies. In addition to this it gives the notion of statistical methods to be applied for having valid and reliable results of the study.

- It throws light on the recommendations of previous scholars, teachers mentioned in their studies for further research.

- A study of related literature was taken by the investigator to get an insight into the work that has already been conducted. The investigator has gone through few studies conducted in India and abroad related to the present study.

Studies related on E-Resources

Mir & Parray (2018) conducted research study on Internet Usage and Academic Performance: An Empirical Study of Secondary School Students in Kashmir. The study revealed that majority of users were female students and they excelled the male students on academic performance. It was also revealed that female students were using internet for communication and educational purposes. Male students were found using the Internet for entertainment and relaxation more than female Internet user students.

Jankiraman & Subramaniam (2015) conducted a survey to find the Awareness in usage of E- resources among users at Agricultural

College and Research Institute, Madurai. The study revealed that majority of users were aware of available e-resources and the electronic resources subscribed by the library were used effectively. The study revealed that 80.6% Postgraduate students and 93.3% Faculty members were making use of freely available e-resources through internet using search engines whereas 70% Ph.D. scholars preferred the use of e-journals. The findings of the study also revealed that digital resources available through CeRA, e-books, Springer link, CABI, Wiley and Black, resources subscribed by the library were widely used by the respondents.

Roopa & Krishnamurthy (2015) conducted a study on Analysis of Digital Library Services at Engineering Colleges in Karnataka. The study revealed that libraries were subscribing more e- journals as compared to e-books. The majority of 97.3% librarians had supported and encouraged the users to use online lecture notes. The institutional repository facility had been provided by 57.3% libraries. For the maximum utilization of digital information resources the information search service had been provided by the libraries. However online chat service, subject portals service, frequently asked questions and instant messaging service had been provided by minimum number of institutions.

Singh and Khan (2015) conducted a study on User' Attitude towards Electronic Resources in IIT Libraries: An Evaluative Study. The study revealed that majority of users visited the libraries web sites and used the library resources and services. The study further revealed that the users preferred the electronic format as compared to print format. The study revealed that e-resources were preferred by the users because these resources are easy to access, relevant and more information is retrieved and save the time. The most of the users preferred to use search engines and library portals to search the information. The majority of Undergraduate and Postgraduate users preferred to use blogs, social networking sites, e-mail and current journals while the Research Scholars and Faculty preferred to access back volumes and current issues of e-journals and e-thesis.

Nwabueze and Urhiewhu (2015) conducted a study on Availability and Use of Digital Information Resources by Undergraduates of University in Delta and Edo States, Nigeria. The study revealed that majority of digital information resources is available in the university libraries in Delta and Estates. The study further revealed that the problems like epileptic power supply, inadequate number of computers, inadequate bandwidth, network problems, and lack of skills to access the digital information resources and lack of formal training on internet use made the low use of digital information resources in all the university libraries.

Kwadzo (2015) conducted a study on Awareness and Usage of Electronic Databases by Geography and Resource Development Information Studies Graduate Students in the University of Ghana in which it was revealed that 96.9% students were aware of electronic databases. The majority of students were aware of JSTOR, Ebscohost, Emerald and Science Direct databases and were making use of these databases for their studies and research. The study revealed that majority of students (68.8%) mentioned that their source of knowledge was their lecturers whereas 62.5% mentioned that they came to know about e-databases from Library website. The majority of respondents (87.5%) were satisfied with the available electronic databases. The students felt that required information can easily be accessed using electronic databases.

Vijayakumar and Thomas (2014) made a study which highlights the preferences and importance of online resources among teachers and research scholars. The Internet and the Web are constantly influencing the development of new modes of scholarly communication; their potential for delivering goods is quite vast, as they overcome successfully the geographical limitations associated with the print media.

Shorunke and Aboyade (2014) conducted a survey to find the Influence of Electronic Resources Use on Students' Reading Culture in Nigerian universities. The study revealed that the most commonly used electronic resources amongst the students included e-book, e-journal, and e-news. 88.68% respondents used the electronic resources very frequently and 90.57% respondents agreed that electronic resources improved their reading habits. 71.17% respondents agreed that they would like to prefer electronic resources to printed resources. The poor internet connectivity felt by 73.11% respondents is the major hindrance in effective use of electronic resources whereas 46.69% respondents considered that inadequate skill to use e-resources is the major hindrance to make optimum and effective use of electronic resources in the library.

Bhat and Mudhol (2014) studied the knowledge and use of Digital Resources by Medical College Students of Govt. Medical College Jammu. The findings showed that 55.63% of the respondents were familiar with the digital resources and used e-mails (39.37%) and internet (34.38%) on daily basis. The study revealed that 71.25% respondents' used digital resources to collect subject specific information and 49.37% respondents agreed that adequate information can be obtained using digital resources. The majority of respondents used the digital resources for communication, to collect information on specific subject, for research and to update their knowledge. But the respondents found it difficult to access resources because of lack of training and time.

Garg and Tamrakar (2014) in their study on Utilization of Electronic Resources by Postgraduate Students, Research Scholars and Faculty members of Indian Institute of Technology, Kharagpur depicted that e-journals were preferred by the respondents as compared to other resources. The majority of users (63.10%) showed the awareness of e-journals and databases available in the library on the subjects of their study/ research. 45.15% of the respondents mentioned that they get the required information from the e-journals. 57.28%respondents mentioned that they get benefited from the e-alert service provided by the library on regular basis. The 52.66% respondents mentioned that the library asked them their information requirements before selecting there sources for the library. 40.53%

of the respondents agreed that the e-service provided by the library helped in study and research.

Kumar and Reddy (2014) conducted a survey to find out the Use of E-Journals by the Research Scholars of Sri Venkateswara University, Andhra University and University of Hyderabad. The study showed that 73.03% research scholars used e-journals for their research work. The majority of respondents, i.e. 64.52%, preferred the use of e-journals for research work but 54.61% respondents still considered print journals as more important as compared to e-journals. The majority of research scholars (73.64%) were satisfied with the search engines. The respondents felt that lack of familiarity with searching e-journals and slow internet connectivity are the major problems in accessing the e-journals. The majority of research scholars still felt that the required information is more available in print journals as compared to e-journals.

Msagati (2014) conducted a study on Use of E-Journals by members of Academic Staff of the Dares Salaam University College of Education (DUCE). The study revealed that 94.4% respondents were interested in using scholarly electronic journals, 86.2% respondents mentioned that they used search engines on daily basis to search the required information. The majority of respondent (i.e. 89.7%) mentioned that the purpose of using e-journals is for writing research proposal. The respondents agreed that lack of training is the major hindrance in effective utilization of e-journals.

Padma et.al. (2014) conducted a case study of two engineering colleges of Tamil Nadu to find the Awareness and Use of Electronic Resources by the Engineering Students. The findings revealed that 86.67% of the respondents were aware of the electronic resources and 81.33% of the respondents used the electronic resources. 39.34% respondents preferred the use of E-journals. 32.79% of the respondents used the electronic resources regularly. 43.33% of the respondents come to know about resources from friends. 35.33% of the respondents use the electronic resources for research work.

29.33% of the respondents use the electronic resources to save the time. 34.67% of these respondents found that lack of facilities is the problem faced by them in using e-resources. 23.33% of the respondents found use of e-resources save the time. 54.67% of the respondents found that electronic resources are important. 46.67% of the respondents were satisfied with the use of electronic resources.

Rani and Chinnasamy (2014) in their study on Users Satisfaction of E-Resources and Services in Self-financing Colleges found that only 37.5% users made use of e-resources for study purpose, 30.6% users made use of resources to improve teaching abilities and only 11.1% respondents used resources for research work. The respondents opined about use of digital library are moderate whereas as far as ICT infrastructure facilities are concerned they opined good. The majority of students preferred to use OPAC, bibliographic data, online searches and full text resources.

Sivathaasan, Murugathas and Chandrasekar (2014) conducted a survey on medical students and academic staff to identify the Impact of Usage of E-Resources on Academic Teachers. The findings revealed that attitude of academic staff and students is different in the use of electronic information resources whereas gender wise and age group wise there is no difference in the attitude of respondents towards the use of electronic information resources.

Tyagi (2014) in the article Analytical Study of Usage of Electronic Information Resources at Pharmacopoeia Libraries in India stated that electronic information resources are the widely accepted means of information resources in the present information society. The scientists of the Pharmacopoeia libraries considered that the latest comprehensive and up to date information which is essential to carry out research can only be obtained using electronic information resources. The scientists of these libraries preferred the use of subject topical websites, e-journals, online databases, e-monographs, CD-ROM databases and standards. The study showed that majority of scientists of these libraries considered electronic information resources as better substitute to get the updated information than printed material.

Ajayi, Shorunke and Aboyade (2014) conducted a survey to find the Influence of Electronic Resources Use on Students' Reading Culture in Nigerian universities. The study revealed that the most commonly used electronic resources amongst the students included e-book, e-journal, and e-news. 88.68% respondents used the electronic resources very frequently and 90.57% respondents agreed that electronic resources improved their reading habits. 71.17% respondents agreed that they would like to prefer electronic resources to printed resources. The poor internet connectivity felt by 73.11% respondents is the major hindrance in effective use of electronic resources whereas 46.69% respondents considered that inadequate skill to use e-resources is the major hindrance to make optimum and effective use of electronic resources in the library.

Adeniran (2013) conducted a study Usage of Electronic Resources by Undergraduates at the Redmeer's University Nigeria. The findings of the study revealed that majority of students were aware of various electronic resources available in the university. The study further depicted that the majority of respondents made use of available resources for assignments, research, current awareness, e-mail and news. The respondents were aware of the electronic resources but still the usage of these resources was low because of retrieval of irrelevant information, non-availability of required material, slow speed of internet and lack of search skills. The results depicted that 80.9% respondents agreed that electronic resources had an effect on their academic performance.

Salman and Ajani (2013) in their article Knowledge and Use of Electronic Information Resources by Academics in Colleges of Animal Health, Animal Production and Veterinary Medicine in Nigeria concluded that 97% of the respondents made use of computer frequently and 77% of the users considered that computer knowledge and skill had significant effect on use of electronic resources. The findings depicted that respondents made use of electronic resources mainly for professional activities, research and teaching activities. The inadequate knowledge of e- resources is the major constraint in the use of electronic resources.

Savitha, Jogan, and Veenakumari (2013) conducted a study on Awareness and Usage of Digital Information Sources and Services by PG students of Kuvempu University. The study depicted that students had low level of awareness and usage of digital information sources whereas the respondents had average level of awareness and usage of digital information services. The study further depicted that the final year Postgraduates had more awareness and usage of digital information resources as compared to previous year students. As far as digital information services are concerned the finding depicted that there is no difference in awareness and usage between final year and previous years' Post Graduate students.

Odongo and Obura (2013) conducted a survey on Electronic Information Resources Utilization in Students of Maraca University Library. The study depicted that majority of respondents were aware of electronic information resources and mentioned that electronic information resources provide more information than print formats. The study also revealed that 92% respondents were aware of Electronic information resources; 77% uses the e-resources in the University Library and 57.5% respondents considered that Electronic Information Resources provide a wider range of information.

Jotwani (2013) conducted a study on Library Resources and Services in Indian Institute of Technology. The study revealed that the libraries had adopted web 2.0 to technique to made home page and Web OPAC more interactive. The study revealed that DS pace software had been used by the libraries of IIT Bombay, Kharagpur, Kanpur and Roorkee libraries to create institutional repository whereas IIT Delhi had used e-print software for creating institutional repository.

Das and Pati (2013) in their study on Evaluating the Awareness and Usage of UGC-INFONET Digital Consortium by the Faculty Members: A Case Study of Odisha University concluded that faculty members had enough skills to operate computers to access the information over the internet but the majority of respondents accessed the UGC-INFONET resources thrice a week only spending 6-8 hours per week. The findings of the study further revealed that the purpose of professors and readers to use Digital Library Consortium is for publications, to write articles for conferences and seminars, to guide research scholars whereas the lecturers made use of these resources for self-improvement, publications and teaching. The major problems encountered by the respondents were low internet bandwidth, poor infrastructure and frequent power failure.

Sivathaasan and Velnampy (2013) conducted a study to find out the Effect of Usage of E- Resources on Academic Performance of University Teachers. The study indicated that usage of e- resources had a strong positive association with academic performance of university teachers. The study revealed that the use of e-resources increased with the increase of academic performance.

Habiba and Chowdhury (2012) conducted a questionnaire based survey to find the Usage of Electronic Resources and its Impact on Dhaka University Library users. The findings revealed that 58% of the users used internet frequently; 52% of the users used search engine to find relevant electronic resources on the internet; 54% users made use of electronic resources for learning purpose; 56% users preferred electronic resources for up to date information as compared to other features and 58% of the users were satisfied with the available electronic resources. The major constraints in effective utilization of electronic resources as mentioned by the respondents are the limited access to computers.

Owolabi (2012) conducted a survey to find the Use of Electronic Information Sources by the Faculty Members in Nigerian Universities. The findings of the study revealed that majorities of teachers always made use of electronic information sources for the research purpose. The most preferred electronic information source as mentioned by the respondents is Internet as compared to other Electronic Information Sources, i.e., CD-ROM, Data bases and OPAC. The findings revealed that majority of respondents use the electronic information sources in the office. The low band width is the major constraint in accessing the electronic information sources.

Ikolo's (2010) study on gender difference based on use of electronic resources revealed that the gender digital divide is manifested in the low number of female users of ICTs compared to men.

Patil and Parameshwar (2009) in paper titled "Use of Electronic Resources by the Faculty Members and Research Scholars in Gulbarga University, Gulbarga: A Survey" disclosed the use of electronic resources by the faculty members and research scholars in Gulbarga University. Questionnaire was used as a data collection tool. Study revealed the need to train users in using the electronic resources.

Singh (2009) examines the search pattern of online journals among the faculty members, research scholars and post-graduate students to collect the required data. The study reveals that the majority of users are aware about the availability of online Journals. It was found that many users faced problem when using online journals and that they were interested in undergoing training on the use of online Journals.

Hayati and Jowker (2008) investigated the effects of different features of electronic reference materials on the rate of their adoption. The result of study showed that most effective attributions of electronic reference resources are the ability to facilitate information retrieval, shortening the time of searching and fair cost of resources. The survey's result suggested that users' previous experience and knowledge are often not applicable to new information resources and to take full advantage of electronic resources it is advisable to draw up programs to facilitate their adoption and understanding of them.

Mand and Mukrangara (2007) conducted a study on gender analysis of electronic information resources use reported that gender is associated with the use of e-resources and male postgraduate students were more likely to use electronic resources than female students.

Tsakonas and Papatheodorou (2006), states that "the transition from print to electronic medium apart from resulting in a growth of electronic information, has provided users with new tools and applications for information seeking and retrieval. Electronic resources are invaluable research tools that complement the print-based resources in a traditional library setting."

Chowdhury (2002) in his article Digital Divide: How can Digital Libraries Bridge the Gap stated that the users of developing countries are still deprived of digital library services. The recent digital developments such as subject gateways, digital reference services, free access to e-journals, e- books e-print archives etc enabled the users of developing countries to make use of these digital libraries so that the digital divide can be reduced when the users actually make use of the information for the purpose of making decisions in every aspect of their daily lives.

Bhattacharya and others (2002) in the article "Digital Information Services: Challenges and Opportunities" mentioned that technological and cultural changes have a considerable effect on the digital resource collection of digital information service. The digital library services include Web-OPAC, CD-ROM, Web-Databases, Digital Reference Service, Electronic Document Delivery, Virtual Library Tours, Library Web Sites, Library Portals, Web-based User Education, FAQ, Library Calendar, Web Forms, Bulletin Boards, Discussion Forum and List serves. The digital library services are becoming highly reliable with the advanced information technology techniques.

Ford, Miller and Moss (2001) observed that female tended to experience more difficulty finding information online, feel less competent and uncomfortable using E resources

Crawford and Dave (2000) in their survey on the Use of Electronic Services at Glasgow Caledonian University Library stated that the word processing, sending and receiving e-mail and web browsing is the common activity. The study revealed that 87.5% users used internet for searching, 75% used e-mail and 62.5% used for word processing. The number of users using either CD-ROM databases or online databases was very less as only 18% used CD-ROM databases and only 13% used online databases. Also the information searching had been a minority activity as only 15% used electronic services for information searching. The above review of literature shows that very few studies had been conducted on the IIT libraries. Though some literature had reflected the usage of library services but not much literature is being available on the availability and usage of digital information resources and services. Hence certain gaps exist in the research of various IIT libraries. This study would help to fill a gap while making a comparative study of availability and usage of digital information resources and services in IIT libraries and would certainly improve the existing literature in this field.

Critical Appraisal

The reviewed literature presented above highlight the e-resource use among students at higher level of education. There are relevant research studies reviewed by the investigator. The reviewed literature have highlighted the need and importance of e-resource use and online services facilitated by the university. The findings of the research showed that there is significant difference in gender in the utilization of electronic resources. The findings supports **Ford; Miller and Moss (2001)** work which reported that females tended to experience more difficulty finding information online but these disagree with observation of on the use of electronic resources by postgraduate students of the department of Library and Information Science, University of Abraka who reported that there is high frequency of usage of electronic resources by both male and female postgraduate students. Therefore gender gap in electronic information resources usage is quite negligible.

It was found that majority of university students have preferred to learn through e-resource format than paper or print based format **(Priyadarshini, Jankiraman and Subramaniam, 2015; Singh and Khan, 2015; Ajayi, Shorunke and Aboyade, 2014).** It was also revealed that there is a significant influence of internet usage on academic performance of students **(Mir and Paray, 2018; Sivathaasan and Velnampy, 2013).** Furthermore, the studies have shown that female Internet-user students are using Internet for communication and educational purposes more than their male counterparts **(Mir and Paray, 2018).** Male students were found using the Internet for entertainment and relaxation more than female Internet user students. Hence, there is a gender gap on using the e-resource. No study has been found by the investigator highlighting the rural-urban disparity among students at university level. This represented the research gap and a strong stimulus for the investigator for conducting such kind of study at university level.

METHODOLOGY

Research Methodology is scientific and systematically way to solve the research problems. A researcher has to design his methodology, i.e., in addition to the knowledge of methods/techniques, s/he has to apply the methodology as well. The methodology may differ from problem to problem. Thus, the scope of research methodology is wider. In a way research methodology deals with the research methods and takes into consideration the logic behind the methods we use. Researcher not only need to know how to calculate the mean, the mode, the median or the standard deviation or chi-square, how to apply particular research techniques, but they also need to know which of these methods or techniques are relevant and which are not, and what would they mean and indicate. Researcher also need to understand the assumptions underlying various techniques and they need to know the criteria by which they can decide that certain techniques and procedures will be applicable to certain problems and other will not.

Thus, when we talk of research methodology we not only talk of the research methods but also consider the logic behind the methods we use in the context of our research study and explain why we are using a particular method or technique and why we are not using other methods so that research results are capable of being evaluated either by the researcher himself or by others.

In the present endeavour, the investigator has used the descriptive research method. Descriptive research methods are used when the researcher wants to describe specific behaviour as it occurs in the environment with respect to one or more variables. It involves interpretation, comparison, measurement, classification, evaluation and generalization. All these direct towards a proper understanding solution of significant educational problem.

Population & Sample

The present study has been carried out on the students of various departments of Sonwar, Nowgam I, Nowgam II and Nowgam III campuses of the Central University of Kashmir. The investigator took students of Central University of Kashmir as the population due to operational ease. The study of the entire target population is practically not possible. The impediments which came in studying the entire population are cost, time and other factors. According to **Fox (1969)**, "It is not possible to collect data from every respondent relevant to our study, but only from some fractional part of the respondents. This process of selecting the fractional part is called sampling." Therefore, sampling is an important and crucial part of behavioural research.

The process of drawing out the sample from the population is known as Sampling. It is a technique of selecting a representative part from the population for the purpose of determining characteristics of the population. Sampling is necessary because we usually cannot gather data from the entire population due to large or inaccessible population or lack of resources. Even in relatively small populations, we cannot obtain information from the whole population, to serve the purpose we employ sampling technique, which is the only method used universally to gather data from respondents. It is a method which makes the research feasible within the available resources.

Consequently a sample of 100 students was selected by stratified random sampling technique from the various departments of Central University of Kashmir including both male and female from urban and rural locality.

Tools Used in the Study

Tools are the ways and means to conduct research and conduct of research can be justified through the methods and techniques meant for it. The collected evident is called the data and the tools used for this are called data collecting tools or devices, which is a common phenomenon in the research. These tools help to analyze the responses of the population on related topic. An important aspect of research work is to choose a suitable tool for the collection of data. The tools are the data gathering instruments, upon which the success of the investigator rests a lot. A self-constructed tool was used in the stated research regarding *"Attitude of students towards the use of E-Recourses in Central University of Kashmir.* The investigator collected data from 100 students of various departments of the all the four campuses of Central university of Kashmir. The students include both male and female from urban and rural locality.

Analyses and Interpretation

Analyses and interpretation of the data was carried out with the help of SPSS by using Mean, S.D. and t Test.

ANALYSES AND INTERPRETATION

According to Carter V. Good et al. (1953), "Analysis is a process which enters into research in one form or the other from the very beginning. It may be fair to say that it consists, in general, of two large steps, gathering of data and the analysis of the data, but no amount of analysis can validly extracted from the data, factors which are not present." It is said further, "The process of interpretation is essentially one of stating what the results show. What they mean, what their significance is, what the answer to the original problem is? The data may be adequate, valid and reliable to any extent, but it does not have any worthwhile purpose unless it is carefully edited, systematically classified, scientifically analyzed, intelligently interpreted, and rationally conduced." According to Frances Rummel (1958), "The analysis and interpretation of data involves the objective material in possession of the researcher and his/her subjective reactions and desires to derive from the data, the inherent meanings in their relation to the problem." Analysis and interpretation of data are the two major steps in the research study. The research can be obtained in general of two steps the gathering of data and analysis of the same. The gathered data through the utilization of tools may be inadequate, valid and reliable unless it is fairly organized, systematically analyzed, interpreted and rationally concluded. Analysis consists of studying the tabulated data in order to determine the inherent facts. Data collected by the investigator receives the meaning when they are placed in the process of statistical analysis which provides insight in the into the concerned research problem.

Results

Objective 1. To study the attitude of male and female students towards the use of E-Resources in Central university of Kashmir.

Ho1. There is no significant difference in the attitude of male and female students towards the use of E-Resources in Central University of Kashmir.

Table 1: Showing the Significance of Mean Difference between Male and Female Students of Central University of Kashmir on Attitude towards e-Resource (N=100)

Group	N	Mean	SD	t-value	Level of Significance
Male	43	68.44	6.77	1.57	NS
Female	57	70.43	5.85		

The interpretation of Table 1 shows the significance of mean difference between male and female students of Central University of Kashmir on their attitude towards e-resource usage. It is quite clear in the Table 1 that mean score of male and female students of Central University of Kashmir on attitude towards e-resource use is 68.44 and 70.43 respectively. The standard deviations are 6.77 and 5.85. The obtained t-value is 1.57. As the obtained t-value does not exceed the tabulated t-value (2.59) at 0.01 level of significance. Therefore, both male and female groups do not differ significantly on attitude towards e-resource use. In this way our hypothesis no. 1 which reads as, *"there is no significant difference in the attitude* among male and female students of Central University towards the use of e resources" stands **accepted.**

Objective 2. To study the attitude of rural and urban students towards the use of E-Resources in

Central university of Kashmir.

Ho2. There is no significant difference in the attitude of rural and urban students towards the use of E-Resources in Central University.

Table 2: Showing the Significance of Mean Difference between Rural and Urban Students of Central University of Kashmir on attitude towards e-Resources (N=100)

Group	N	Mean	SD	t-value	Level of Significance
Rural	49	68.06	6.72	2.41	Significant at 0.05 level
Urban	51	71.03	5.57		

The interpretation of Table 2 shows the significance of mean difference between rural and urban students of Central University of Kashmir on attitude towards e-resource use. It is quite clear in the Table 2 that mean score of rural and urban students of Central University of Kashmir on attitude towards e-resource use is 68.06 and 71.03 respectively. The standard deviations are 6.72 and 5.57. The obtained t-value is 2.41. As the obtained t-value exceeds the tabulated t-value (1.96) at 0.05 level of significance. Therefore, both rural and urban groups differ significantly on attitude towards e-resource use. In this way our hypothesis no. 2 which reads as, *"There is no significant difference in the attitude among rural and urban students of Central University towards the use of e resources"* stands **rejected.**

CONCLUSION

The present study is the original and honest work of the investigators to study the "Attitude towards the use of e-resources among the Students of Central University of Kashmir". 100 students were selected randomly from various departments of Central University of Kashmir. A self-constructed tool was used by the investigator to collect the required data. Statistical treatment was done by mean, standard deviation and t-test.

Findings of the Study

- Male and female CUK students do not differ significantly on attitude towards e- resource use.
- Rural and urban CUK students differ significantly on attitude towards e-resource use. Urban students have favored the mean differences.

Discussion

In the present time advancement in computer technology has revolutionized the whole world. The time has gone when students were totally dependent on the spoon-feeding by the teachers. Present education system has taken a new mode in the teaching learning process. The competition is becoming rapid day by day and to compete in this competition especially at higher level of educations students are supposed to be alert, to be step forward from book material only. They are moving towards the new technology, utilizing electronic resources for educational purpose. In the present day scenario, the technological explosion has opened up new vista of learning procedure in the classroom of every institution especially at higher level. The e-resources knowledge helps the students to get self-educated and also interact with their peer group to discuss upon any topic. The present study reveals that there is no difference of gender towards the use of E-Resources. Both male and female students utilize such resources equally. The present educational scenario demands more and more up to date information of the elements so that students can cope up the process of educational system at the best level. Both male as well as female students are well aware about the use of e-resources as they are getting exposure regarding the new technology equally. Both prefer to use electronic information resources than printed stuff.

On the other hand the study reveals that there is significant difference towards the use of E- Resources between urban and rural students. Computer literacy is basic need for using E-Resources and this literacy is poorly found in the rural students. This type of illiteracy in the field of computer keeps rural section of students away from the use of E-Resources. The students from rural environment come with poor learning facilities that do not include online sources. Therefore, such students have not been exposed to information resources and technologies. The urban students use online sources more than their rural counterparts due to their interactive and timeliness features. This provides explanation why rural students are lagging behind urban ones towards the use of E-Resources.

Suggestions

The modern changing IT environment has made its own impact in the field of Library and Information centres and the digital revolution has entered into the libraries. The attention of users has also turned towards the online resources. So it is highly recommended that paper based material or documents of university library should be replaced with digital and online database. Blending learning is also suggested to feed and watered the university students.

The qualities like easy availability, cost effectiveness and latest up-datedness have added the attraction of the online resources among the users. The 'e' resources have been produced in enormous in various forms like 'e' articles, 'e' databases, 'e' journals, etc. Existing information carriers on paper or celluloid like books, journals, microphones tapes, optical devices etc. and their surrogates like secondary or tertiary documents are being converted into computer readable databases gradually to meet the present need of the society. We are moving towards a paperless society for variety of constraints.

To convert the existing library and information systems into digital library system, it is essential to plan it before a switch over. The first and foremost requirement is a strong will to leave the conventional library techniques and to adopt the new information technology for collection development, processing, providing various searching tools, circulation, dissemination, retrieval and maintenance of library material.

Recommendations

Following recommendations of the study are inevitably essential to all education stakeholders.

- Development of infrastructure facilities for accessing electronic resources by the users and to cover all the subjects content of Central University of University, the library should subscribe more e-journals.

- Various orientation programs regarding the use of electronic resources should be provided so that students can get well aware about the ways of utilizing the same.

- Central University of Kashmir should increase the budget for subscribing more electronic resources. Without adequate budget library cannot cover all subjects' content. The e-journal cost is increasing day by day and among those the current issues are more costly than back issues. Most of the CUK student's requirements are current issues of article; some of them told that they no need to see the back issues of e-journals;

- Before and after the electronic resources subscription, survey on users should be done at regular interval. Library should also receive information and suggestions from the faculty members and the students, which need to subscribe or not;

- Various Schools of Central University of Kashmir should organize training program for the faulty members and the students so that they can know about different search interface, latest changes of the journals site and develop sophisticated searching and retrieval skills or techniques;

- Bandwidth of internet connection must be increased in Central University of Kashmir. Faster internet access should be offered to minimize download time.

- Electronic resources should be publicized by the librarians and faculty members as many of the undergraduates and postgraduates are unaware of these e-resources. Library should encourage the users to use open access resources. It is a fact that the value of these resources increases as they are used.

Limitations

Following are the limitations of the present study. (1) The study has included only postgraduate students of Central University of Kashmir. (2) Only 100 students were selected as the sample for the present study. To conclude we can say that there is no significant difference between male and females on attitude towards e-resources while as there is a significant variation among rural and urban students of Central University of Kashmir Students on attitude towards e-resources.

BIBLIOGRAPHY

1. Abouserie H. (2006) Use of electronic journals by Library and Information Science faculty members in performing various academic tasks: a field study performed at the school of information science at the University of Pittsburgh. 'Available at.www.eric.ed.gov

2. Adeniran, Pauline (2013). Usage of electronic resources by undergraduates at the Redeemer's University, Nigeria, International Journal of Library and Information Science, 5(10), 319-324.

3. Agarwal, Umesh Kumar & Dave, Rajesh Kumar (2009). Use of Internet by the Scientists of CAZRI: A survey. *Indian Journal of Library and Information Science,* 3(1), 15-21.

4. Ali NPM, Satyanarayana NR (2002) "Online searching of scientific information: a study of science and technology libraries in Delhi", paper presented at National Conference on Information Management in E-Libraries., Allied Publishers Ltd, New Delhi.

5. Ali, Naushad & Faizul, Nisha (2011). Use of e-journals among research scholars at Central Science Library, University of Delhi. *Collection Building,* 30 (1), 53-60.

6. Angello C (2010). "The awareness and use of electronic information sources among livestock researchers in Tanzania", *J. Inform. Literacy,* 4 (2):6-22.

7. Ansari, M. N. & Zuberi, B. A. (2010). Use of electronic resources among academics at the University of Karachi. *Library Philosophy and Practice,* pp. 4-5. Retrieved from http://unllib.unl.edu/LPP/ansari-zuberi.htm

8. Asefeh, Asemi & Nosrat, Riyahiniya (2007). Awareness and Use of Digital Resources in the Libraries of Isfahan University of Medical Sciences, Iran. *The Electronic Library,* 25 (3), 316-327.

9. Ashok Babu, T. (1998). Modern information technologies: their impact on library services. Indian Journal of Information, Library and Society, 11(3-4), 12-18.Central Library, Indore., pp 309-319.

10. Bharati, M. S. Z. & Zaidi, S. Mustafa (2008). Use of e-journals and e-databases of UGC-Infonet Consortium by faculty members and research scholars of Aligarh Muslim University. Procccdings of the *6th International Caliber-2008,* Allahabad University, Allahabad, 28th -29th Feb and 1st March, 2008 Ahmedabad: INFLIBNET Centre, pp.341-346.

11. Borrego, A. & Urbano, C. (2007). Analysis of the behavior of the users of a package of electronic journals in the field of chemistry. *Journal of Documentation,* 63 (2), 243-258.

12. Borrego, A. et al. (2007). Use and users of electronic journals at Catalan Universities: The results of a survey. *Journal of Academic Librarianship. 33* (1). Retrieved from http://www.agInternetwork.org.

13. Chirra, Rekha & Madhusudhan, Margam (2009). Use of electronic journals by doctoral research scholars of Goa University, India. *Library Hi Tech News*, 26 (10), 12-15.

14. Chopra, H. S. (2008). E-Resources: Vision and Utilization of Case Study of Users of Guru Nanak Dev University, Amritsar (Punjab*). 6th International CALIBER-2008*, University of Allahabad, Allahabad, pp. 621-625.

15. Dalgleish A, Hall R (2000), "Uses and perceptions of the World Wide Web in an information-seeking environment", *J. Library Inform. Sci.*,32 (3):104–16.

16. Devendra Kumar (2010). Faculty Use of Internet Services at a University of Agriculture and Technology. Library Philosophy and Practice (E-Journal) http://digitalcommons.unl.edu/cgi/viewcontent.cgi?article=1330&context =libphilprac

17. Devi VC (1996), "Attitude of the end-users towards online information retrieval – A case study of NSDRC library, Vishakpatanam", Annals of Library Science and Documentation, Vol. 44 No.1 pp.18-31.

18. Dilek-Kayaoglu, Hulya (2008). Use of electronic journals by faculty at Instanbul University, Turkey: The results of a survey. *The Journal of Academic Librarianship,* 34 (3), 239-247.

19. Dubai International Academic City (2012). Indian Universities Dubai, UAE (2012). Available at: http://www.diacedu.ae/academic-partners/indian-universities/

20. Eason, K., Richardson, S. and Yu, L. (2000), "Patterns of use of electronic journals", Journal of Documentation, Vol. 49 No. 4, pp. 356-69.

21. Ekwelem, V. O., Okafor, V. N. & Ukwuoma, S. C. (2009). Students' use of electronic information sources at the University of Nigeria, Nsukka. *African Journal of Library, Archival, and Information Science*, 7 (1), 34-45.

22. Ellis, D. (1989), "A behavioural approach to information retrieval system design", Journal of Documentation, Vol. 45, pp. 171-212

23. Faizul, Nisha, Ali, Naushad & Ara, Tabassum (2008). Use of INDEST and UGC-INFONET E-Journal Consortia: A Comparative analysis. In From Automation to Transformation. *Proceedings of CALIBER,* held at University of Allahabad, Allahabad, February 28-29 & March 1, 2008. Allahabad: INFLIBNET, 2008: 3.24-3.29.

24. Forsman RB (1998). "Managing the electronic resources transforming research libraries: challenges in the dynamic digital environment", Advances in Librarianship, 22(1):1–19.

25. Galyani, Moghaddam & Talawar,V.G (2008). The use of Scholarly Electronic Journals at the Indian Institute of Science: a case study in India. *Interlendings Document supply,* 36 (1), 15-29.

26. Gomez, E. & Others (2007). Utilizing Web Tools for Computer-Mediated Communication to Enhance Team-Based Learning. *International Journal of Web-Based Learning and Teaching Technologies*, 2 (2), 21-37.

27. Gowda, V., and Shivalingaiah, D., (2009). Attitude of research scholars towards usage of electronic information resources: A survey of university libraries in Karnataka, Annals of Library and Information studies, 56 (3) 184-191.

28. Gupta, Vibha (2008). Use and accessibility of e-journals by Ph.D. students in University of Lucknow: a survey. Proceedings of the *6th International Caliber-2008*, Allahabad University, Allahabad, 28th -29th Feb and 1st March, 2008. Ahmedabad: INFLIBNET Centre, pp. 569-582.

29. Henderson T, Machewan B (1997). "Electronic collections and wired faculty", Library Trends, Vol. 45 (3):488–98.

30. Jansen BJ (2000). "The effect of query complexity on web searching results." Inform. Res, 6(1):12-23.

31. Joteen, R. K., Singh, Madhuri Devi & Raychaudhury, Arup (2009). Use of internet based e-resources at Manipur University: a survey. *Annals of Library and Information Studies,* 56 (1), 52-57.

32. Kamba M. A. (2009). Problems, Challenges and Benefits of Implementing E-learning in Nigerian Universities: An Empirical Study. *IJET*, 4 (1), 653.

33. Kanniyappan, E., Nithyanandan, K. & Rivichansran, P. (2008). Use and Impact of e-resources in an Academic and Research environment: a case study. *Kelpro Bulletin,* 12 (1), 27-36.

34. Kaur, Baljinder & Verma, Rama (2009). Use and impact of electronic journals in the Indian Institute of Technology, Delhi, India. *Electronic Library,* 27 (4), 611–622.

35. Kaur, Baljinder &Verma, Rama. (2009) Use of Electronic Information Resources: A Case Study of Thapar University. DESIDOC Journal of Library & Information Technology, 29(2), 67-73.

36. Khan, A. M., Zaidi, S. M., Zaffar, & Bharati, S. (2009). Use of on-line databases by faculty members and research scholars of Jawaharal Nehru University (JNU) & Jamia Millia Islamia (JMI), New Delhi (India): A

survey. *The International Information & Library Review*, 41 (2), 71-78. Retrieved from http://www.sciencedirect.com.

37. Khan, Abdul Mannan, Zaidi, S. Mustafa and Bharati, Md. Safay Zaffar (2009). Use of on-line databases by faculty members and research scholars of Jawaharlal Nehru University (JNU) and Jamia Millia Islamia (JMI), New Delhi (India): A survey. *The International Information & Library Review*, 41(2): 71-78.

38. Khan, M. Shamsul Islam (2009). Electronic Information Resources: Access and Use. Digital information system, July 28th, 2009. http://infosciencetoday.org/digital-information-system/electronic-information-resources-access-and-use.html

39. Kumar, Ashok, Saravanan, N. T. & Balasubramani, R. (2008). Users attitude measurement towards e-resources in Madras University library. *Library Progress (International)*, 28 (1), 1-9.

40. Kumar, G. T. & Kumar, B. T. Sampath (2008). Use of electronic information sources by the academic community: A comparative study. *6ᵗʰ International CALIBER-2008*, University of Allahabad, Allahabad. pp. 684-692.

41. Lau, S. & Woods, P. C. (2008). An investigates for user perception and attitudes towards learning objects. *British Journal of Educational Technology*, 39 (4), 685-699.

42. Madhusudhan, M. (2008). Use of UGC Infonet – journals by the Research Scholars of University of Delhi. *Library Hi Tech*, 26 (3), 369 – 386.

43. Madhusudhan, Margam & Aggarwal, Shalini (2011). Web-based online public access catalogues of IIT libraries in India: an evaluative study. *Library and Information Sciences- Computer Applications*, 54 (4), 415-438.

44. Majid S, Abazova AF (1998). "Computer literacy and use of electronic information sources by academics: a case study of International Islamic University, Malaysia", Asian Libraries, 8(4):100–11.

45. Malik, Satish Kumar, (2007) Web based information resources; a case study of Electronic Journal, ILA Bulletin, 43 (2) 31-35.

46. Naidu GHS, Rajput Prabhat & Motiyani Kavita, Use of Electronic Resources and Services in University Libraries: A Study of DAVV University

47. Naqvi Shehbaz Husain, Use of Electronic Resources at Jamia Millia Islamia (A Central University): A Case Study, In: NACLIN 2007, p320-324.

48. Natarajan, K., Suresh, B., Sivaraman, P. & Sevukan, R. (2010). Use and user perception of electronic resources in Annamalia University, India: A case study. *Annals of Library & Information Studies,* 57 (1), 59-64.

49. Okello-Obura, C. & Magara, E. (2008). Electronic Information access and utilization by Makerere University in Uganda. Retrieved from http://creative commons.org/licenses/by/2-0.

50. OlubankeMofoluwaso, Bankole, BosedeAdebimpe, Ajiboye, Aderonke O Otunla (2015). Use of Electronic Information Resources By Undergraduates Of Federal University Of Agriculture, Abeokuta, Ogun State, Nigeria. International Journal of Digital Library Services, 5(4), 1-14.

51. Priyadharshini, R., Janakiraman, A., Subramanian, N. (2015). Awareness in usage of e-Resources among users at Agricultural College and Research Institute, Madurai: A case study, European Academic Research, 2 (2) 14816- 14823.

52. Rao, Y. Srinivasa & Choudhury, B. K. (2009). Availability of Electronic Resources at NIT Libraries in India: A Study. ICAL, 2009, Poster papers, 630-636.

53. Rasool-abadi, Masood (2007). Kordesstan Medical Science Faculty Members' Awareness Level with Search Skills and search Strategies in the Internet. *Nama, electronic Journal of Irandoc*, 2.

54. Raza, Masoom M. & Upashyay, Ashok Kumar (2010). Use of e-journals by researchers: A comparative study. *International Journal of Library Science,* 2 (A 10), 52-63.

55. Salako, O. A. & Tiamiju, M. A. (2007). Use of search engines for research by Postgraduate students of the University of Ibadan, Nigeria. *African Journal of Library, Achieves and Information Science,*7 (2), 103-115.

56. Satpathy SK, Rout B. Use of e-resources by the faculty members with special reference to CVRCE Bhubaneswar. DESIDOC J Libr Inf Technol 2010;30:11-6.

57. Satpathy, Sunil Kumar & Rout, Biswanath (2010). Use of E-Resources by the faculty members with special reference to CVRCE, Bhubaneswar. *DESIDOC Journal of Library and Information Technology,* 30 (4), 11-16.

58. Selim H. M. (2007). Critical success factors for e-learning acceptance: confirmatory factor models, Computer & Education. 49 (2), 396-413.

59. Sharma, Chetan (2009). Use and impact of e-resources at Guru Gobind Singh Indraprashta University (India): a case study. *Electronic Journal of Academic and Special Librarianship,* 10 (1), Retrieved from http://southern librarianship.icaap.org/content/v10n01/sharma_c01.html.

60. Shukla, Praveen & Mishra, Rajini, (2011). Use of e-resources by Research Scholars of Institute of Technology Banaras Hindu University, India. *Journal of Arts, Science and Commerce.* Retrieved from http://www. researchchersworld.com/vol2/issue2/Paper_17.pdf.

61. Singh, B., Kapila, P. C. & Pateria, R. (2007). University libraries in digital environment: vision 2020. *ILA Bulletin,* 43(3), 5-12.

62. Singh, K. P., Sharma, N. & Negi, N. (2009). Availability, use and barriers to ICT in the R&D institutions: a case study of the libraries and information Centres in Noida. *DESIDOC Journal of Library & Information Technology,* 29 (6), 21-31.

63. Stanford University (2002) e Just: e-journal user study, Stanford University. http://ejust.stanford.edu/.

64. Sujathan, H. R. & Mudhol, V. (2008). Use of Electronic Information Sources at the college of fisheries, Mangalore: India. *Annals of Library and Information Studies,* 55 (3), 234-245.

65. Tyagi S (2012). "Use of Electronic Information Resources at the Indian pharmacopoeia Commission", DESIDOC Journal of library and Information Technology, 32 (2):171-78.

66. Tyagi, Sunil. (2011). Use and Awareness of Electronic Information Sources at IIT Roorkee, India: A Case Study, Journal of Library and Information Science, 2(1), 4586-21. doi: 10.4403/jlis.it-4586.

67. Upadhyay, Navin & Chakrabarty, Hearakant (2008). Online journals and databases: a study of use and awareness among academics at Main Library, I.T., B.H.U. Proceedings of the *6thInternational Caliber-2008,* (pp. 648-655) Allahabad University, Allahabad, 28th -29th Feb and 1st March, 2008. Ahmedabad: INFLIBNET Centre.

68. Veenapani, S., Singh, Khomdon & Devi, Rebika (2008). Use of e-resources and UGC-INFONET Consortium by the teachers and research scholars in Manipur University. Proceedings of the *6th International Caliber-2008,* Allahabad University, Allahabad.

69. Vishala, B. K. & Bhandi, M. K. (2008). Use of UGC-INFONET digital library consortium resources. Proceedings of the *6thInternational Caliber-2008,* Allahabad University, Allahabad, 28th -29th Feb and 1st March, 2008. Ahmedabad: INFLIBNET Centre, 583-596.

70. Walmiki, R. H. & Ramakrishnegowda, C. K. (2009). ICT infrastructure in university libraries in Karnataka. *Annals of Library and information studies,* 56, 236-241.

APPENDIX 1: QUESTIONNAIRE

School of Education, Central University of Kashmir

ATTITUDE OF STUDENTS TOWARDS USE OF E-RESOURCES IN CENTRAL UNIVERSITY OF KASHMIR

Dr. Ismail Thamarasseri, Research Supervisor & Qurat Ul Ain, 4th Sem. M.A. Education Student

Dear Student,

The following Questionnaire has been prepared to assess the Attitude of Students towards use of E-resources in Central University of Kashmir. Please read the below statements and give your responses. Your responses will be kept confidential, so you are requested to respond to the statements without any bias.

Personnel Details:

Name	
University Enrolment No.	
Department	
Gender	Male/Female
Locality	Urban/Rural

S. No.	Statements	Strongly Agree	Agree	No Opinion	Disagree	Strongly Disagr
1	I am aware about E-Resources					
2	E-Resources are easy to access					
3	E-Resources save my time					
4	Computer literacy is important for one to use E- Resources					
5	I prefer E-Resources rather than print material.					
6	There are very few online resources available in my subject					
7	The use of E-Resources will improve my academic performance					
8	I prefer E-Resources because they are available 24x7 mode					
9	There is lack of orientation for the use of E-Resources					
10	It takes lot of time to get relevant data while accessing E-Resources					
11	I use E-books for recreational purpose					
12	It has become my habit to read E-books					

13	E-Resources are expensive than printed resources					
14	Many titles that are available in traditional text books are not available on E-Resources					
15	I am aware that CUK library provides access to E-Books.					
16	E-books are positive alternation for traditional learning way.					
17	E-Resources has removed my ability to browse library shelves.					
18	I use E-Resources to do my class assignments.					
19	I use E-Resources to update my knowledge about the subjects I am interested					
20	I consider the use of E-Resources in the library as wastage of time.					

www.ingramcontent.com/pod-product-compliance
Lightning Source LLC
Chambersburg PA
CBHW031231050326
40689CB00009B/1555